This Journal is Dedicated to:

_____

_____

_____

I dedicate this journal to you, with sincere appreciation for your commitment to finding joy amidst life's stresses. By taking the time to focus on what you are grateful for, you are actively fostering a positive and resilient mindset that can help you navigate life's challenges. It is my hope that this journal will serve as a reminder of the many blessings that surround us, even in difficult times.

May these pages serve as a source of comfort and inspiration, helping you to embrace gratitude as a way of life and find joy in the present moment. Through gratitude, we can shift our focus from what we lack to what we have, and cultivate a greater sense of fulfillment and happiness. Thank you for joining me on this journey towards greater positivity and appreciation.

With gratitude,
Rohan Richardson

Everyday
Gratitude
Your Journey to Joy

"Everyday Gratitude: Your Journey to Joy" is a personalized journal that helps you track your progress towards a more joyful and appreciative life. With dedicated space to reflect and record your thoughts and experiences, this journal is your companion as you strive towards happiness.

Scientific research shows that gratitude can significantly improve our happiness and well-being. When we focus on the positive aspects of our lives, even in difficult times, we cultivate a more positive outlook. By practicing gratitude, we can shift our attention away from negative thoughts and appreciate the good things in our lives. This can lead to an overall improvement in our satisfaction and well-being.

This journal facilitates a daily gratitude practice. Each day, prompts allow you to reflect on what you are grateful for and to consider ways to bring more joy into your life. By taking the time to reflect on your gratitude each day, you can cultivate a positive mindset and build a foundation of appreciation.

Brace yourself for an introspective journey. Let us delve into the transformative power of gratitude and embark on a path towards a life filled with joy and contentment.

How to Use This Journal

Start by noting the current date and writing for a few minutes each day. This simple practice can quickly bring you feelings of relief, joy, and positivity. To enhance your journaling experience, we have included the following elements.

PROMPTS

To make your journaling more effective, be sure to date each entry and use prompts that help you reflect on important and even minor details of your life that you may miss regularly. As you write, remember to pause and express gratitude for the people, experiences, or things that you appreciate.

AFFIRMATIONS

Affirmations can help you stay positive and optimistic. You can repeat them to yourself whenever you need to change your way of thinking. The journal entries are quick and designed to cultivate gratitude. Eventually, you'll naturally start feeling more gratitude in your everyday life. This journal is here to help you become a more thankful person, regardless of why you want to improve. Let's explore how gratitude can make life better!

FUN CHALLENGES

Weekly challenges promote positive habits for daily routine. Design challenges for personal growth, like trying new healthy recipes or practicing meditation. Include challenges in journaling to feel accomplished and create momentum toward enhancing well-being.

INSPIRATIONAL QUOTES

You'll encounter quotes from wise individuals who integrate gratitude into their lives. These diverse perspectives offer insight into the essential role gratitude plays in a happy, healthy, and fulfilling life.

EXTRAS

Throughout the journal, there are pages available for you to further express yourself. Whether you want to sketch, brainstorm, or simply expand upon your gratitude reflections, these pages are here to help you do so in your unique way. Enjoy this extra space and make it your own.

MON TUE WED THU FRI SAT SUN   Date: _____

Today, I am grateful for:

_____

_____

_____

_____

I am capable and deserving of love and happiness.

Something that makes me smile...

_____

_____

_____

Highlight of the day...

_____

_____

_____

_____

Help someone who may be going through a tough time.

I feel so blessed that...

_____

_____

_____

_____

I am worthy of success and abundance.

A beautiful reason to be happy right now:

_____

_____

_____

Today, I accomplished...

_____

_____

_____

_____

MON   TUE   WED   THU   FRI   SAT   SUN   Date: _____

Gratitude is not only the greatest of virtues, but the parent of all the others.

— Cicero

Today, I am delighted to have:

_____

_____

_____

_____

My uniqueness is a strength and I should celebrate it.

Someone I get to spend time with today...

_____

_____

_____

Things that made today a little better...

_____

_____

_____

_____

Write a letter to a loved one expressing your appreciation.

Today, I feel fortunate to have:

_____

_____

_____

_____

I have the power to change my life and create my own reality.

A quality of a loved one that I appreciate:

_____

_____

_____

_____

What made today awesome:

_____

_____

_____

_____

MON TUE WED THU FRI SAT SUN   Date: _____

Today, I am grateful for:

_____

_____

_____

_____

I am a resilient and strong individual.

A song that always brings me joy:

_____

_____

_____

One of my most treasured memories:

_____

_____

_____

_____

Indulge in your favorite hobby

I feel fortunate to have:

_____

_____

_____

_____

I am enough just as I am, right now.

Someone I get to speak with today:

_____

_____

_____

What made today a special day:

_____

_____

_____

_____

MON TUE WED THU FRI SAT SUN   Date: _____

Today, I am honored to have:

_____

_____

_____

_____

My feelings are valid and deserve respect.

Someone that makes my life better by being in it:

_____

_____

_____

A valuable lesson I learned from a difficult situation:

_____

_____

_____

_____

Take a few minutes each day to meditate or practice deep breathing.

I am blessed to have:

_____

_____

_____

_____

I have the ability to overcome any challenge and obstacle.

One of the best parts about being me:

_____

_____

_____

I enjoyed myself today because...

_____

_____

_____

_____

─────── GRATEFUL GIST ───────

Gratitude is the fairest blossom which springs from the soul.

Henry Ward Beecher

I feel so fortunate to have...

_____
_____
_____
_____

My talents can make a positive impact on the world.

A skill that I possess which I appreciate:

_____
_____
_____

Moments that brought me joy and happiness today:

_____
_____
_____
_____

Cook your favorite meal this week

I'm filled with appreciation for...

_____
_____
_____
_____

I am deserving of love, kindness, and compassion.

An influential person in my life:

_____
_____
_____

My highlight of today:

_____
_____
_____
_____

MON TUE WED THU FRI SAT SUN   Date: _____

I'm deeply appreciative of...

_____

_____

_____

_____

I have the potential to achieve great things.

A fragrance or aroma that brings me to my happy place:

_____

_____

_____

A moment that has helped me to appreciate life more:

_____

_____

_____

_____

Spend time outside each week, whether it's going for a walk or having a picnic.

It means a lot to me that...

_____

_____

_____

_____

I have the ability to love deeply and be loved in return.

My favorite thing about my job:

_____

_____

_____

Today was a great day because....

_____

_____

_____

_____

MON TUE WED THU FRI SAT SUN   Date: _____

I'm so glad to have...

_____

_____

_____

_____

My thoughts and opinions matter and are important.

A hobby the brings me great joy:

_____

_____

_____

A special part of today was...

_____

_____

_____

_____

Date: _____

Do something kind for a stranger this week.

I feel so fortunate to have...

_____

_____

_____

_____

I trust in my own abilities and am confident in my decisions.

A movie/series that I love to binge and why:

_____

_____

_____

My day was awesome because...

_____

_____

_____

Draw Something

MON TUE WED THU FRI SAT SUN   Date: _____

Gratitude can change the pangs of memory into a tranquil joy.

Deepak Chopra

Today, I am grateful for:

_____

_____

_____

_____

I am deserving of a fulfilling and happy life.

What I love about my home/apartment:

_____

_____

_____

What I discovered about myself today:

_____

_____

_____

_____

My Gratitude

A hardship or difficulty that I have faced and the lessons or growth that I gained from it.

_____

_____

_____

_____

_____

_____

_____

_____

_____

_____

_____

_____

_____

_____

_____

_____

_____

_____

_____

_____

_____

Forgive someone who has wronged you, and let go of any resentment

I'm thankful for...

_____

_____

_____

_____

I am strong and resilient, no matter what challenges come my way.

Someone who makes me feel safe:

_____

_____

_____

Today was memorable because...

_____

_____

_____

_____

MON TUE WED THU FRI SAT SUN   Date: _____

Gratitude is the best medicine. It heals your mind, you soul, and your body.

— Louise Hay

I feel so lucky to have...

_____

_____

_____

_____

I choose to focus on the positive and let go of negativity.

What I appreciate about my morning routine:

_____

_____

_____

What made me happy today:

_____

_____

_____

Approach your challenges as opportunities to learn and grow

I'm thankful for...

_____

_____

_____

_____

I am grateful for all that I have in my life.

What I appreciate about my current living situation:

_____

_____

_____

What I did today was...

_____

_____

_____

GRATEFUL GIST

Happiness is not a destination, it is a journey. And the journey itself is home.

Shunryu Suzuki

Today, I am grateful for:

_____

_____

_____

_____

I am constantly learning and growing, becoming the best version of myself.

Two things that I love about my job:

_____

_____

_____

Today's experiences...

_____

_____

_____

_____

Do something nice for a stranger, like holding the door open or offering a smile.

I'm thankful for...

_____

_____

_____

_____

I am a unique and amazing individual, with so much to offer the world.

A memory that makes my heart glad:

_____

_____

_____

One thing I learned today:

_____

_____

_____

_____

MON TUE WED THU FRI SAT SUN   Date: _____

Today, I am grateful for:

_____

_____

_____

_____

I am strong and capable of overcoming any obstacle.

A favorite place that brings me joy...

_____

_____

_____

I practiced gratitude for the small things today by...

_____

_____

_____

_____

Think of something that you usually take for granted, and imagine how life would be without it.

I'm thankful for...

_____

_____

_____

_____

I choose to let go of negative thoughts and focus on positivity.

The main thing I love about my spiritual practice:

_____

_____

_____

I overcame an obstacle today by...

_____

_____

_____

_____

GRATEFUL GIST

The best and most beautiful things in the world cannot be seen or even touched - they must be felt with the heart.

— Helen Keller

Today, I am delighted to have:

_____

_____

_____

_____

I am grateful for all the blessings in my life.

The main thing I love about my community is...

_____

_____

_____

I took time to appreciate the beauty in the world today by...

_____

_____

_____

_____

Offer to teach a friend or family member a new recipe or cooking technique that you love.

I'm thankful for...

_____

_____

_____

_____

I am surrounded by abundance and prosperity.

What I enjoy most about my morning coffee/tea:

_____

_____

_____

I showed empathy towards others by...

_____

_____

_____

_____

MON TUE WED THU FRI SAT SUN   Date: _____

Joy is not a feeling of happiness. Joy is a spiritual attribute that produces a feeling of happiness.

—— Rick Warren ——

Today, I am grateful for:

_____

_____

_____

_____

I choose to see the good in every situation.

One thing you appreciate about reading/writing is...

_____

_____

_____

I celebrated a success, or achievement today by...

_____

_____

_____

_____

Spend time in nature, like going for a hike or visiting a park

I'm thankful for...

_____

_____

_____

_____

I am at peace with myself and the world around me.

Three things I love about my partner

_____

_____

_____

I practiced forgiveness today by...

_____

_____

_____

MON TUE WED THU FRI SAT SUN   Date: _____

Today, I am grateful for:

_____

_____

_____

_____

I am open to new experiences and opportunities.

A place that makes me feel calm....

_____

_____

_____

I made progress in overcoming a challenge today by...

_____

_____

_____

_____

Reflect on the best day you've had in a week and write about what made it special.

I'm thankful for...

_____

_____

_____

_____

I believe in myself and my dreams.

The aspect of nature that I find most calming:

_____

_____

_____

Today was an awesome day because...

_____

_____

_____

_____

GRATEFUL GIST

Joy is not in things; it is in us.

— Richard Wagner

Today, I am grateful for:

_____

_____

_____

_____

I am free from self-doubt and self-criticism.

What I am thankful for about my family...

_____

_____

_____

I identified and challenged negative self-talk today by...

_____

_____

_____

_____

Practice mindful meditation today to cultivate a state of awareness

I'm thankful for...

_____

_____

_____

_____

I am always learning and growing as a person.

Someone who has shown me unconditional love and support

_____

_____

_____

I practiced mindfulness or meditation today by...

_____

_____

_____

_____

MON TUE WED THU FRI SAT SUN   Date: _____

Today, I am deeply appreciative of:

_____

_____

_____

_____

I am loved and valued for who I am.

A coworker or classmate who has been helpful in the past:

_____

_____

_____

My accomplishments for today:

_____

_____

_____

_____

Take a moment to reflect on your daily routine and express gratitude for the things you enjoy doing.

I'm thankful for...

_____

_____

_____

_____

I am worthy of a life filled with purpose and meaning.

The quality that I look for in a good book:

_____

_____

_____

I made progress towards a long-term goal today by...

_____

_____

_____

_____

Draw Something

GRATEFUL GIST

Gratitude turns what we have into enough.

Melody Beattie

Today, I am grateful for:

_____

_____

_____

_____

I am capable of achieving my goals and reaching my full potential.

One book that I'm thankful for:

_____

_____

_____

I ended the day feeling satisfied and fulfilled because...

_____

_____

_____

_____

My Gratitude

A moment when I felt grateful for the love and support of my family.

_____

_____

_____

_____

_____

_____

_____

_____

_____

_____

_____

_____

_____

_____

_____

_____

_____

_____

_____

Give someone a heartfelt, genuine compliment that speaks to their character or personality.

I'm thankful for...

_____

_____

_____

_____

I am worthy of success and abundance.

What I appreciate most in my favorite animal:

_____

_____

_____

Today was special to me because...

_____

_____

_____

_____

MON TUE WED THU FRI SAT SUN   Date: _____

Be the change you wish to see in the world.

Mahatma Gandhi

Today, I am grateful for:

_____

_____

_____

_____

I am surrounded by supportive and loving people.

What I appreciate about my evening routine:

_____

_____

_____

How I expressed my feelings effectively today:

_____

_____

_____

_____

Offer to mentor or tutor someone who could benefit from your expertise or guidance.

I'm thankful for...

_____

_____

_____

_____

I choose to focus on solutions rather than problems.

The part of travelling that I enjoy the most:

_____

_____

_____

I treated others with kindness and respect by...

_____

_____

_____

_____

MON TUE WED THU FRI SAT SUN   Date: _____

Gratitude is the most exquisite form of courtesy.

Jacques Maritain

Today, I am grateful for:

_____

_____

_____

_____

I am capable of creating the life I want.

A recent accomplishment that I am proud of:

_____

_____

_____

I practiced patience and understanding with someone today by...

_____

_____

_____

_____

Reflect on a past mistake or failure and express gratitude for the lessons learned

I'm thankful for...

_____

_____

_____

_____

I am filled with courage and inner strength.

The quality that I look for in my good friend:

_____

_____

_____

I practiced self-reflection today by...

_____

_____

_____

_____

MON TUE WED THU FRI SAT SUN   Date: _____

Gratitude is a powerful catalyst for happiness. It's the spark that lights a fire of joy in your soul.

— Amy Collette

Today, I am grateful for:

_____

_____

_____

_____

I am kind to myself and others.

A mentor who has helped me:

_____

_____

_____

Today, I learned...

_____

_____

_____

_____

Write about a time when someone gave you a compliment and how it made you feel.

I'm thankful for...

_____

_____

_____

_____

I am a unique and special individual.

The aspect of music that I find most inspiring:

_____

_____

_____

I stepped out of my comfort zone when...

_____

_____

_____

_____

─── GRATEFUL GIST ───

Gratitude is an opener of locked-up blessings.

Mary Mullen

Today, I am grateful for:

_____

_____

_____

_____

I trust in the universe to guide me on my path.

A memory that brings me happiness:

_____

_____

_____

I ended the day feeling satisfied and fulfilled because...

_____

_____

_____

*Listen actively and respond with empathy when someone is
telling you about their struggles or challenges.*

I'm thankful for...

_____

_____

_____

_____

I am a magnet for positivity and good things.

The thing that I appreciate most about my favorite restaurant:

_____

_____

_____

I inspired or motivated someone today by...

_____

_____

_____

_____

GRATEFUL GIST

The most important thing is to enjoy your life - to be happy - it's all that matters.

Audrey Hepburn

Today, I am grateful for:

_____

_____

_____

_____

I am proud of myself and my accomplishments.

What I appreciate about my physical abilities:

_____

_____

_____

Today, I felt proud of myself for...

_____

_____

_____

_____

Plan a surprise party or gathering for someone you appreciate, just to show them how much they mean to you.

I'm thankful for...

_____

_____

_____

_____

I am proud of myself for how far I've come

The trait that I value most in a coworker:

_____

_____

_____

What made today a productive one:

_____

_____

_____

_____

Believe you can and you're halfway there

Theodore Roosevelt

Today, I am grateful for:

_____

_____

_____

_____

I am living a life of purpose and fulfillment.

What I appreciate about history:

_____

_____

_____

Today, I felt amazing because...

_____

_____

_____

_____

Give someone a hug or a high-five to show your appreciation or congratulations.

I'm thankful for...

_____

_____

_____

_____

I choose to let go of the past and embrace the present moment.

What I appreciate most about my home country:

_____

_____

_____

My thoughts on today's activities:

_____

_____

_____

_____

MON TUE WED THU FRI SAT SUN   Date: _____

Don't watch the clock; do what it does. Keep going

Sam Levenson

Today, I am grateful for:

_____

_____

_____

_____

I am healthy and strong in body, mind, and spirit.

A friendship that I cherish is....

_____

_____

_____

I challenged myself today by...

_____

_____

_____

Offer to help a neighbor with yard work, cleaning, or other tasks that they might need assistance with.

I'm thankful for...

_____

_____

_____

_____

I am creating a life that I love and that makes me happy.

A colleague who motivates me to strive for success:

_____

_____

_____

I worked collaboratively with others today by...

_____

_____

_____

_____

MON TUE WED THU FRI SAT SUN   Date: _____

Today, I am grateful for:

_____

_____

_____

_____

I am confident in my abilities to achieve my goals and dreams.

My favorite memory of a dear family member:

_____

_____

_____

Today was a good day simply because...

_____

_____

_____

_____

*Send a handwritten note or card to someone you haven't seen
in a while, just to say hello and express your gratitude.*

I'm thankful for...

_____

_____

_____

_____

I am deserving of love, respect, and kindness.

A place I would like to visit, and why:

_____

_____

_____

Today, I was able to accomplish...

_____

_____

_____

_____

Draw Something

GRATEFUL GIST

Gratitude is the memory of the heart

— Jean Baptiste Massieu

Today, I am honored to have:

_____

_____

_____

_____

I am deserving of a healthy and active lifestyle

The main thing I love about my favorite snack:

_____

_____

_____

The reason today was awesome....

_____

_____

_____

_____

MON TUE WED THU FRI SAT SUN   Date: _____

My Gratitude

Expressing my gratitude while reflecting on the people who have helped me in
my career or education.

_____

_____

_____

_____

_____

_____

_____

_____

_____

_____

_____

_____

_____

_____

_____

_____

_____

_____

_____

Offer to run an errand or pick up groceries for someone who is unable to do so themselves.

I'm thankful for...

_____

_____

_____

_____

I am worthy of success and achievement.

A charity or cause I support, and why:

_____

_____

_____

One thing that made my day today:

_____

_____

_____

_____

MON   TUE   WED   THU   FRI   SAT   SUN   Date: _____

The more you cultivate joy, the more joy you will experience

Eckhart Tolle

Today, I am grateful for:

_____

_____

_____

_____

I am capable of manifesting my desires

What I appreciate about my career:

_____

_____

_____

Today, I was able to...

_____

_____

_____

_____

*Offer to listen to someone who needs to talk, without judging
or trying to solve their problems.*

I'm thankful for...

_____

_____

_____

_____

I am filled with gratitude for all the blessings in my life.

Three things I'm grateful for about my health:

_____

_____

_____

I tackled a difficult task successfully today by...

_____

_____

_____

_____

GRATEFUL GIST

Happiness is not something ready made. It comes from your own actions

Dalai Lama XIV

Today, I am grateful for:

_____

_____

_____

_____

I am at peace with myself and those around me.

Three things I appreciate about my family:

_____

_____

_____

Today, I made time for self-care by...

_____

_____

_____

_____

Send a care package or surprise gift to someone who could use a pick-me-up.

I'm thankful for...

_____

_____

_____

_____

I am constantly growing and evolving into the best version of myself.

My favorite memory of my grandparents:

_____

_____

_____

Today was a great day simply because...

_____

_____

_____

_____

MON TUE WED THU FRI SAT SUN   Date: _____

Find joy in everything you choose to do. Every job, relationship, home… it's your responsibility to love it, or change it

— Chuck Palahniuk

Today, I am grateful for:

_____

_____

_____

_____

I choose to see the beauty in everything and everyone.

Three things I look forward to in the future:

_____

_____

_____

Today, I enjoyed my time doing…

_____

_____

_____

_____

Write a positive review or testimonial for a business or service that you appreciate.

I'm thankful for...

_____

_____

_____

_____

I am free to be myself and express my true self.

Why I love my favorite ice cream

_____

_____

_____

To improve my day, I could have done differently by...

_____

_____

_____

_____

GRATEFUL GIST

Gratitude is the single most important ingredient to living a successful and fulfilled life

— Jack Canfield

Today, I am grateful for:

_____

_____

_____

_____

I am open to receiving all the good things the universe has to offer me.

Things that made me smile today:

_____

_____

_____

I took steps towards achieving my goals by...

_____

_____

_____

_____

Share a skill or talent that you have with someone who could benefit from it.

I'm thankful for...

_____

_____

_____

_____

I am filled with positive and uplifting energy.

Three things I love about my mysel:

_____

_____

_____

I overcame an obstacle today by...

_____

_____

_____

_____

GRATEFUL GIST

The most important thing is to enjoy your life - to be happy - it's all that matters.

Audrey Hepburn

Today, I am grateful for:

_____

_____

_____

_____

I am worthy of all the love and happiness that life has to offer.

The trait that I admire most in a person:

_____

_____

_____

Something that went right today:

_____

_____

_____

_____

Make a donation to a charity or cause that someone you know cares about.

I'm thankful for...

_____

_____

_____

_____

My mind is filled with positive and empowering thoughts.

What I love most about road trips:

_____

_____

_____

I practiced self-reflection today by...

_____

_____

_____

_____

GRATEFUL GIST

Gratitude is the way to bring more into your life

— Les Brown

Today, I am grateful for:

_____

_____

_____

_____

Joy and positivity flow through me and into the world around me.

A friend who always knows how to make me laugh:

_____

_____

_____

The main thing that I learned today:

_____

_____

_____

_____

Cook a meal or bake a treat for a friend or family member to show your appreciation.

I'm thankful for...

_____

_____

_____

_____

Every day is a new opportunity to learn and grow.

A person who inspires me to be a better version of myself:

_____

_____

_____

I received feedback today and responded by...

_____

_____

_____

_____

MON TUE WED THU FRI SAT SUN   Date: _____

Today, I am grateful for:

_____

_____

_____

_____

The possibilities for my life are endless and exciting.

Someone I get to spend time with today:

_____

_____

_____

I showed kindness and compassion to others today by...

_____

_____

_____

_____

Give someone a compliment or express your gratitude for their positive qualities.

I'm thankful for...

_____

_____

_____

_____

Opportunities come easily and naturally to me.

Someone who has taught me a valuable skill or hobby:

_____

_____

_____

I overcame an obstacle today by...

_____

_____

_____

_____

MON TUE WED THU FRI SAT SUN   Date: _____

There is always something for which to be thankful.

Nelson Mandela

Today, I am grateful for:

_____

_____

_____

_____

My mind is clear and focused, and I am always making progress towards my goals.

A family member who has taught me important life lessons:

_____

_____

_____

I handled difficult situations calmly and rationally by...

_____

_____

_____

_____

Offer to help someone with a task or project without expecting anything in return.

I'm thankful for...

_____

_____

_____

_____

My heart is open to all of the beauty and love in the world.

A neighbor who has become a close friend:

_____

_____

_____

I expressed gratitude towards others by...

_____

_____

_____

_____

Notes

In this great future, you can't forget your past.

Bob Marley

Today, I am grateful for:

_____

_____

_____

_____

I am a powerful force for good in the world.

An aspect of nature that I find most beautiful:

_____

_____

_____

I communicated effectively with others by...

_____

_____

_____

Notes

Buy a small gift or treat for a friend or loved one just because you're grateful for them.

I'm thankful for...

_____
_____
_____
_____

I am deserving of forgiveness and self-forgiveness

A recent act of kindness I experienced:

_____
_____
_____

I learned something new about myself today when...

_____
_____
_____
_____

GRATEFUL GIST

The more grateful I am, the more beauty I see

Mary Davis

Today, I am grateful for:

_____

_____

_____

_____

I am full of potential and possibility.

Type of music that brings me joy...

_____

_____

_____

Today was special to me because...

_____

_____

_____

_____

Write a thank-you note or send a text message to someone who has helped you recently.

I'm thankful for...

_____

_____

_____

_____

I am worthy of a successful and fulfilling career.

A reminder of the beauty in my life:

_____

_____

_____

What I learned today...

_____

_____

_____

_____

MON TUE WED THU FRI SAT SUN   Date: _____

Today, I am grateful for:

_____

_____

_____

_____

I am deserving of a healthy and active lifestyle.

A reason to smile right now

_____

_____

_____

Today, I was able to accopmish...

_____

_____

_____

_____

Share a book or article that you found helpful or inspiring with someone who could benefit from it.

I'm thankful for...

_____

_____

_____

_____

I am strong and resilient in the face of challenges.

A musician that I enjoy listening to and why:

_____

_____

_____

I made progress towards a long-term goal today by...

_____

_____

_____

_____

MON TUE WED THU FRI SAT SUN   Date: _____

Today, I am grateful for:

_____

_____

_____

_____

I am deserving of forgiveness and self-forgiveness.

A person who has helped me in difficult times:

_____

_____

_____

One thing that went well today:

_____

_____

_____

_____

Leave a positive comment or review on someone's social media page or blog.

I'm thankful for...

_____

_____

_____

_____

I am a confident and capable problem-solver.

What I enjoy about my school/work life:

_____

_____

_____

I made a positive impact on someone's life today by...

_____

_____

_____

_____

MON TUE WED THU FRI SAT SUN   Date: _____

There is no greater joy than feeling indebted.

Today, I am grateful for:

_____

_____

_____

_____

I am worthy of self-care and relaxation.

What I appreciate about art or other forms of expression:

_____

_____

_____

What made my day wonderful was...

_____

_____

_____

_____

*Share a meaningful experience or memory with someone, and
express how grateful you are to have shared it with them.*

I'm thankful for...

_____

_____

_____

_____

I am deserving of peace and happiness in all areas of my life.

Someone who has been a constant source of support for me:

_____

_____

_____

What made today awesome...

_____

_____

_____

_____

MON TUE WED THU FRI SAT SUN   Date: _____

He who does you a kindness will never forget it, and he who wrongs you will never remember it.

Arabic Proverb

Today, I am grateful for:

_____

_____

_____

_____

I am capable of manifesting my desires.

The attribute I find most important in a teammate:

_____

_____

_____

My accomplishments for today:

_____

_____

_____

_____

Take a moment to reflect on your daily routine and express gratitude for the things you enjoy doing.

I'm thankful for...

_____

_____

_____

_____

I am a positive and optimistic person.

What I appreciate about rainy days:

_____

_____

_____

The highlight of my day was...

_____

_____

_____

_____

MON TUE WED THU FRI SAT SUN   Date: _____

We can only be said to be alive in those moments when our hearts are conscious of our treasures

Thornton Wilder

Today, I am fortunate to have:

_____

_____

_____

_____

I am surrounded by supportive and loving people.

The aspect of fashion that I find most intriguing:

_____

_____

_____

What I did today...

_____

_____

_____

_____

Challenge yourself and explore a new venue, or try a new dish

I'm thankful for...

_____

_____

_____

_____

I am deserving of a balanced and fulfilling life.

The thing that I love about my culture:

_____

_____

_____

What I learned about myself today was...

_____

_____

_____

_____

MON TUE WED THU FRI SAT SUN Date: _____

────────── GRATEFUL GIST ──────────

A grateful mind is a great mind, which eventually attracts to itself great things.

— Plato

Today, I am grateful for:

_____

_____

_____

_____

I am full of positive energy and enthusiasm.

What I love most about being at a concert:

_____

_____

_____

The most exciting thing that happened to me today was...

_____

_____

_____

_____

Practice self-care to improve your mood and energy

I'm thankful for...

_____

_____

_____

_____

I am worthy of self-care and relaxation.

What I love about watching the sunset:

_____

_____

_____

The best part of my day was...

_____

_____

_____

_____

MON   TUE   WED   THU   FRI   SAT   SUN   Date: _____

Today, I am grateful for:

_____

_____

_____

_____

I am a capable and confident decision-maker.

What I love most about family gatherings:

_____

_____

_____

One thing that went well today:

_____

_____

_____

_____

Congratulations !!

Congratulations on completing your gratitude journal! You have taken an important step towards cultivating a positive mindset and embracing a grateful attitude.

By taking the time to reflect on the things you are thankful for each day, you have opened your heart and mind to a world of blessings.

As you reflect on your journey, remember that gratitude is not just an activity, but a way of life. You can integrate this practice into your daily routine, helping you to focus on the good in your life and appreciate the blessings that surround you.

In closing, I encourage you to keep the spirit of gratitude alive in your heart. Take a moment each day to reflect on the things you are thankful for and express your appreciation to those around you. Let gratitude be your guide and watch as your life becomes filled with joy, peace, and abundance.

Thank you for taking this journey with me. May this journal serve as a reminder of all the wonderful things in your life, and may you continue to cultivate a grateful heart for years to come.

With gratitude,
Rohan Richardson

Notes

Notes

Notes

Notes

Made in United States
Troutdale, OR
09/04/2023

12623982R00060